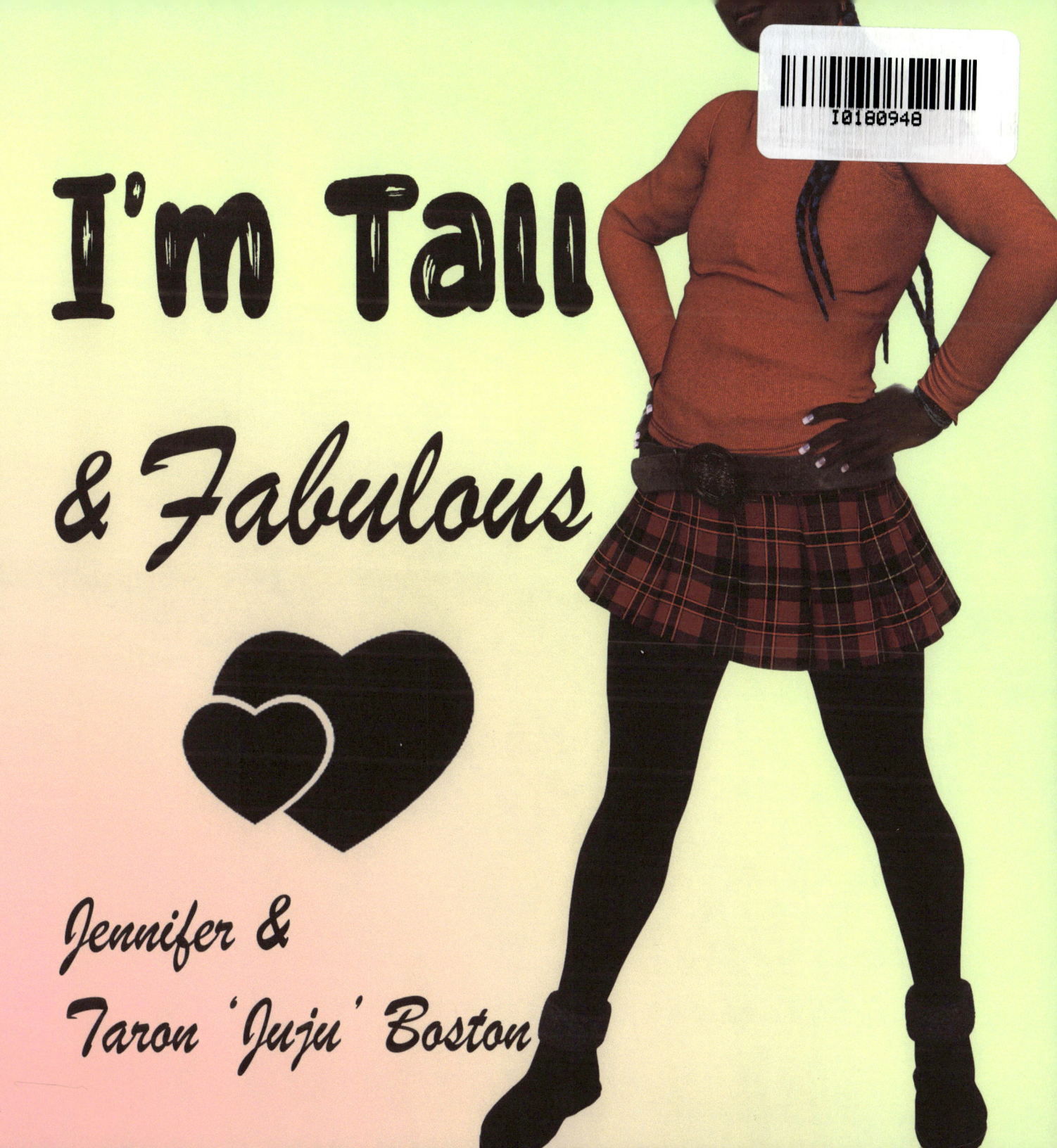

I'm Tall & Fabulous
Copyright (C) by Jennifer & Taron 'Juju' Boston 2023
All Rights Reserved

Some images (c) Big Stock Photo, Daz3D

ISBN: 979-8-218-14930-7
Independently Published

To My Nu,

You're perfect in every way! Never forget.

Love Always,
Mom xoxo

People come in all shapes and sizes.

This is something we all should know.

So why do people go out of their way to remind me when I grow?

I've been called a tree, a ladder, and a giraffe, too.

Would it be appropriate to respond,

"At least I'm not as short as you?"

If I did such a thing, I'm certain my mom would be called.

But I'm a human. I have feelings. Why can't we all just get along?

Tree Girl

Too Tall

Giraffe

Giant

It's not just kids.
Adults are guilty too.

One time, a kid was so mean about my height and even kicked my leg.

I was asked if my legs got cold at night, and how's the weather up there?

This kid misbehaved.

Fed up, I called my mom at work and asked her to come get me.

I'm usually able to block the haters...

...but this day, my self-esteem I couldn't trust.

As soon as we got in the car, I broke down in tears.

I told Mom I'm usually strong, but the weight

of the teasing
I could no longer bear.

Mom pulled the car over, reminded me I was beautiful, made in God's perfect image that she adored.

She said,
"I'm turning this car around. We're going back. Being bullied will not be ignored!"

When we arrived back at camp, Mom explained the ordeal to the present staff.

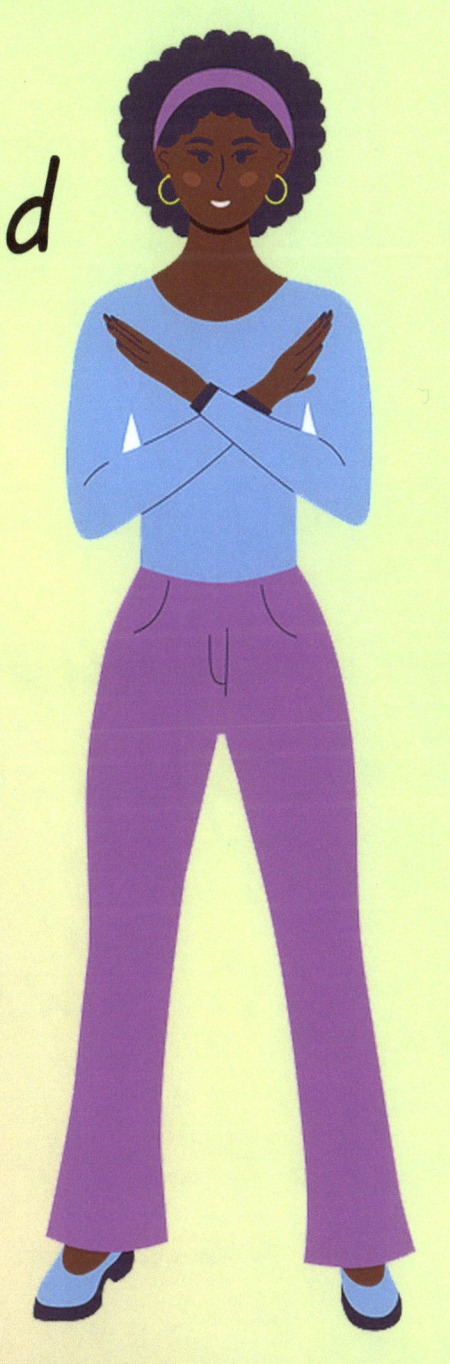

They rounded up the kids to explain the rules and that they wouldn't tolerate kids being bad.

Over the next several days, Mom shared lots of information on the joys of being tall.

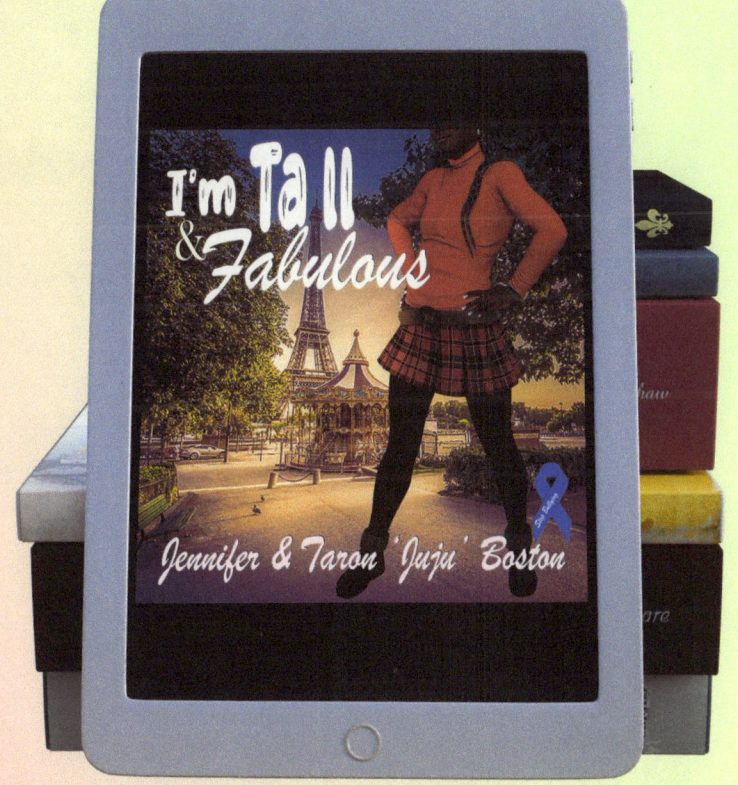

It helped me regain my confidence. I felt victorious, thinking, "Here I come, world, tall and all!"

I remembered I'm tall and fabulous when I'm doing gymnastics, cheering, swimming, riding a skateboard, and posing with friends too!

Even when I'm riding camels past the Great Pyramid of Giza in Egypt and posing in front of the Eiffel Tower with my crew!

To the tall kids in the world that might feel down when others make fun of you:

Remember your greatness, your amazing attributes. It's just a phase, all very temporary, so keep going.

I see you shining, boo!

A Word from the Authors

Love yourself,
wholeheartedly, unapologetically.

Shoulders back, head up.

Smile! The world is yours!

Other Books by Jennifer & Juju

Join 5-year-old Juju on her adventures as she travels the world with her family!

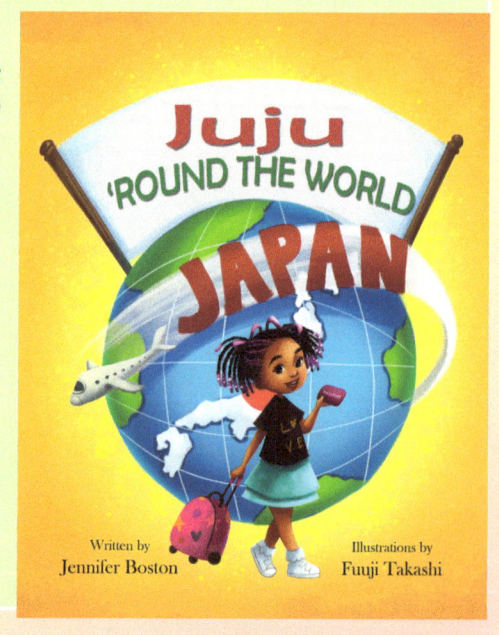

"Don't Touch Me" details Juju's account of being violated by a former deacon of the Roman Catholic Diocese of Albany, a convicted child molester that evaded his prison sentence and sex offender registration due to 'slipping through the cracks' of the New York judicial system. Connected through family ties, Juju bravely shared the account with her mom which resulted in conviction. To date, no one in the judicial system has taken responsibility.

From scared and unsure to brave and courageous, Juju and her mom share intimate details of a tragedy transformed to triumph.

About the Authors

Jennifer Boston was born and raised in the projects of NYC. A high school dropout at age 15, she received her GED from Job Corps at the tender age of 16. By the age of 20, she joined the United States Army, where she acquired a new outlook on life.

A single mom by the age of 22, she left the military and later returned to school. Within 5 years, she earned an associate's, bachelor's, and master's degree with honors. In 2017, she self-published her first children's book, "Juju 'Round The World" in five languages, which takes you on the journey of relocating her family from Atlanta, GA, to Japan for her new career post-college from her daughter's perspective. They enjoyed living in Japan and Germany, which afforded them the opportunity to travel abroad to several countries throughout Asia, Europe, and Africa.

Currently residing in Cuba, she enjoys giving back to communities globally, while encouraging everyone she encounters to "live their best life" despite their circumstances. She believes in the power of positive affirmations #IAM

Taron "Juju" Boston is 11 years old and enjoys life abroad. Courageous and adventurous, Juju can be found jumping into the deep end of the pool with friends, zip lining through obstacle courses, and making jewelry.

www.jujuroundtheworld.com - jb@jujuroundtheworld.com
InstaGram: juju_round_the_world - Facebook: Juju 'Round the World

www.ingramcontent.com/pod-product-compliance
Lightning Source LLC
LaVergne TN
LVHW072116070426
835510LV00002B/72